T0065262

# LET ME GET USED TO THIS

# LET ME GET USED TO THIS

## Real Thoughts

# LET ME GET USED TO THIS

*iUniverse books may be ordered through booksellers or by contacting:*

*iUniverse*
*1663 Liberty Drive*
*Bloomington, IN 47403*
*www.iuniverse.com*
*844-349-9409*

*Because of the dynamic nature of the internet, any web addresses or links contained in this book may have changed since publication and may no longer be valid. The views expressed in this work are solely those of the author and do not necessarily reflect the views of the publisher, and the publisher hereby disclaims any responsibility for them.*

*Any people depicted in stock imagery provided by Getty Images are models, and such images are being used for illustrative purposes only. Certain stock imagery © Getty Images.*

*ISBN: 978-1-6632-0678-7 (sc)*
*ISBN: 978-1-6632-0677-0 (e)*

*Library of Congress Control Number: 2020922122*

*Print information available on the last page.*

*iUniverse rev. date: 12/09/2020*

# CONTENTS

# PREFACE

At the age of eight, I started writing short stories of people and situations I saw or was around. After I would finish writing, I would give the story to the people who it was about, and the response that I would get was "That's nice." Most of the time, the stories were dark and very gory for an eight-year-old to write.

So, I switched it up and started writing poetry. Since the age of eight, poetry has always been my go-to, to release what is inside me. Now at the age of twenty-nine, I feel that the world needs real poetry for everyday life and situations. Poems that will give you mental visions of what you should feel while reading my poetry.

The world should finally get to know the caged bird that is always seen and not heard. My poetry is real with fictional characters—some real, some made up. This is just a little interlude to many realities through my eyes. Enjoy!

# ACKNOWLEDGMENTS

God is the reason for everything and all that's creative, including artistry in every aspect of the universe. Thank you to my grandfather (father) for allowing me to be myself. Thank you to my grandmother for being my biggest fan, and my mother for always being there in a time of need. Thank you to my Auntie Chelle for teaching me to do things on my own. Thank you to my cuddy for always being a listening ear. Thank you to every friend and family member who always knew I would be something greater than myself.

Thank you to the people who are just waiting for me to fail. I hope you hate what I have to say just as much as you like to hate everything I do. To my lovely Queen, I thank you and appreciate you for helping me align my chakras and helping me heal. To disbelievers and naysayers, fuck you.

To every source that gets to read and rate this piece of art, thank you for giving me an opportunity to share a taste of what I have always wanted to say but just feel. Feel free to take quotes and make memes for the conscious folks; I'm here for it. Feast your eyes on my creative way to unleash words that are unspoken thoughts of love, pain, passion, and life. Sit back and relax. After this, there's more to come.

# CAGED BLACK BIRD (PART 1)

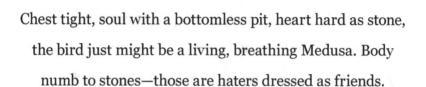

Chest tight, soul with a bottomless pit, heart hard as stone, the bird just might be a living, breathing Medusa. Body numb to stones—those are haters dressed as friends. Paranoia decided to be its best friend, sitting beside the bird with caution. Its mind is open to new things, but its anxiety told me about its abandonment issues, who hired construction workers to build glass walls 'cause it needs to see red flags. It's fucked up; but its mysterious vibe attracts the bird's loneliness. Sometimes, it'll invite visitors to come see a young black bird in a cage trimmed in gold with locks of dreams with the keys of hope hanging outside of the cage.

Fascinated by the bird writing down a get-out plan. Hanging strategies on the bars—that keeps the flash out when posers wanna snap pics and use its name in vain. Maybe it's because the bird's intimacy is good; you can tell by the glow that shines off the black bird's coat.

So it's screaming, "Let me out." It already lost its loyalty circle. This black bird just wants to be free so it can fly free. I guess the Lord needs the strongest and the survivors to live through shit. I guess that black bird is surviving to be better. Well, anxiety switched seats with paranoia. Testing the black bird's ability to break the locks, instead of using the keys of hope, it used a bat of fear made up of bricks of anger, but its progress is only whispering encouragement. The bird smokes trees of Bob Marley; that's when it feels gnarly, building courage to break free. Breaking free is kinda harder when it's the only one locked up, and instead, people are watching and not helping, and it's having to weave out genuine souls because its spirit is putting in overtime, pushing the caged bird to beat harder. I guess with all that anger and aggression that the bird has, maybe one day, someone will pass by and see the hard beating that it's giving the cage and give it the keys of hope, but shit, by that time, the caged bird will break out; so I guess in due time.

# AMUSING

Amazingly drawn to her vibe, this dark-skinned lotus flower bomb got this Leo tamed at her leisure. What's chivalry if you've never experienced it? I can assure you my generosity is completely genuine. I'm the last of a dying breed, and you give me the inspiration that gives me the energy to write my true feelings on paper again. I been doing this shit for a minute, and all my poems sounded like fire after I said hi to you. Maybe it's because all of them now are about you. Baby, you're the bomb. Just call me Bryson Tiller, writing songs about his ex. Just know if we don't work, my poems and books will have your influence just so you can be a part of American history. Lately I haven't been on your good side, so my world is dark. My days are unsure of happiness and despair. I need your smile to be the light to light up my day, but what am I worth to you if I can't make you smile? Maybe my demons have already scared you away 'cause three years ago, you wouldn't have even looked my way, 'cause I let the ugly side of me run wild. So, *Child's Play* for me now is a good movie. I've played my part, written scripts about the point of the game; it didn't give me fame, only pain so I can learn how to love genuinely. And just like my sex, love has no different effect. Intense and interesting, my sex amazes the closed-minded but intrigues the open-minded. So, I don't need you to be blinded by my shortcomings. Words and actions are different but take effect the same. Only one of them is short-lived. So amuse me with your light to let me know you still are intrigued by my intellect, because my intentions have already been shown and proved I need you. So, what do you need me for? Dry conversations only lead to second-guessing of what's supposed to be an assured thing. You're ... Amusing ... My muse ... Don't know what it is? I'll show you, but you gotta stay amusing to my eye, and the fact that you don't see what I see when I look at you is perfect; I can show you. Only if you let me. I'll give you spare time by yourself only if you show me your thoughts of me.

# IN A-MAZE-MENT

Caught in a whirlwind, fascinated by your desire to string my

heart along as you figure out where to hang it. Don't know if

I'm coming or going unless you provide me with the location.

So as my mind is draped with thoughts of wonder and second-

guessing, should I stay, or should I go? You pull me back into

the light just enough for me to close the door on another.

So, I'm trapped. In a-maze-ment. Filled with

a garden of black and blue roses

(that's how my heart colors itself when it's near you) just to

hide in silence and put my soul on an appearance on a stage

of tortured feelings, dying to get a signed autograph of your

plan to confuse the best part of me that I keep to myself.

So I'll dance in my despair in this maze that you've led me to,

as amazed as I am that you have the power to keep me here

with no ball and chain to attack me from walking away.

I wish I could make a movie with the emotions that you give me, but they just don't fit well with the script of the feelings that I know I thought you would have. This situation to me is a-maze-ment. I'm working for your acceptance so one day I can hold the key to your heart, but I'm afraid that even if I'm able to hold the key, it'll only be a hologram. So instead, I'll try to find my way out because I deserve better, but your smile and kisses are the curse that I cannot find a spell for. I'm stuck in this maze. So I've built a Ferris wheel to overlook the ocean filled with beautiful mermaids that I would love to touch, but my hands seem to enjoy touching you, only when you allow me to. I'm tamed at your leisure, so I'm sacrificing my world just to sit with you in a car with no wheel to steer; so if we crash, it's okay. I'll take the blame 'cause at the end of the day, it's your a-maze-ment that keeps me near.

# NOW OR NEVER

Come with me and take a flight to ecstasy that brings our two worlds together. Creating a space and time for our love to be forever. Sharing possibilities and options for the day that we say, "I do." I choose to paint your thoughts on the ceiling of my bedroom, but the color scheme isn't as perfect as the outline of your dreams. So as my character gets familiar with your actions that are not coy with your bitterness, I build a church for you to hold its funeral and write my signature for its cremation. I'm lost with the endless bliss of looking into your eyes. How beautiful they are when the sun hits them and gives me hopes and fantasies to become your wife. It's now or never. Bleeding endlessly of paranoia that you'll leave, I'm becoming more in tune to our happily-ever-after, where our kids grow up to see love at its best. So, it's now or never; I would take that leap with you knowing that our flaws are still being worked on. I guess you have the recipe for our love to grow and not die. So, let's do this now because *never* doesn't fit into *I do.*

# I LOVE WOMEN

Fell asleep with Jada on my mind; she gives me peace of mind in my slumber. She quotes positive and private thoughts in my ear just so she can feel my appreciation. Woke up to Sanaa Lathan rubbing my back 'cause my front was occupied by Zoe Kravitz giving me knowledge, and the way she lets me write my notes in class provides the power I need to handle Lisa Ray. Now, me and Ms. Ray have our ups and downs; she can't seem to grasp why I still like going to strip clubs so much. But she's a queen—hell, all of them are. I love women; might be a gift and a curse, but let Angela Bassett tell it while I'm feeding her grapes that I'm a real one. Gentlewoman. Had to go give some attention to Megan Fox 'cause even though she's a fox, she'll act like one if I don't stroke her often. Funny thing is she sometimes forgets that I'm a woman by the way her body shakes while I'm hitting her from the back. She likes her coffee with caramel, and I like mine with a little bit of cream, but my sugar is Kehlani. She gets my tree; chop it up and roll it up before I pull up 'cause she knows I'm gonna be a distraction. My day won't go good if I can't work out Meagan Good at the gym; that is, she helps me keep my body looking sexy for her. I love women, but it might be a gift and a curse. Heard Regina King was looking for a queen. So, I bought her a chariot to glide her to my world and sit her on a throne that she can't refuse. I used to let girls break my heart, but my poetic thoughts are so strong; Janet gives me justice to find a woman who can handle this Leo. Now in the wintertime, Chilli gives me chills while I'm always burning up talking green with Beyonce (dead presidents, that is), and even though Kelly keeps me rolling, it's Michelle who keeps me grounded; maybe that's why I'm so humble for Kerry Washington. I love women; can't you see? And even though this is my own fantasy, I'll still create a pace to chase Nia 'cause I have been loving her a long time.

# CRYPT TONIGHT

Sat in the house the other day cleaning my Glock 40—oh,
I mean my mind—clearing the thoughts of you being the
tiger to my anger, but maybe it was just the mere thought of
you believing in my downfall. Checking my calendar of the
struggle for my story 'cause I'm still young. Even the greatest
gotta be dirty before they drip in pure gold, so I take a shower
in His glory and praise the Most High for what I got.
Keep your childish statements in a glass case with the trophies
of negative motivation. Keep my arm vertically to your chest;
keep a smile on my face. But I really want to punch you in
the face for the false hope of connecting on a different level.
Maybe I was just too emotional. Maybe I couldn't have cared
as much stretching the thought of you actually loving me.
A broken diamond that shines bright at your disposal.
Separating love within pushing-out grins for the actual
reaction to make-believe everything is okay. I guess that's

how you remain nonchalant with a fluent essence of you

reminiscing on how your life could have been. Drama-

free laugh, love, joy, and pain 'cause without pain, there's

no reason to fall. So, my deception is a pattern.

"To fuck with you, or not to fuck with you?" It's a puzzle 'cause

I need the least part that no one pays attention to, and that's

your humanity and the curiosity to find out what love really is.

In fact, your mentality forbids the feeling of loving genuinely;

instead, it rather grasps the pure thought of what buys and what

makes the outside happy. So what is my position in your life?

Am I just a fuck or the friend kept tucked tight in your

bosom? Using a chisel to brand a print of your place on my

heart. Only giving me the time that you sat aside to fuck

with me. I guess my vibe is just that divine to be felt but not

embraced. I'm a bitter rack draped in a robe of depression,

but you're not the cause; you're part of the why factor. So,

I'm chasing time to find the real me. Trying to dig deep

to say no to you, but it is a bridge that my heart will not

allow me to burn, so my mind is the guard that only prefers

two steps at a time at the moment 'cause my trust for you

has altered, and the elephant in the room knows it.

With a trunk blowing out the truth every five minutes,

why are we here? Sharing space and time, creating

memories that are questionable to even remember. But at least it's nice for the moment. So, let's leave words unspoken, and let our actions be broken into movements. 'Cause with you, I'm drowning, but without you, I have no gravity to keep me from reaching the bottom.

# WISHFUL THINKING

I wish I could strip your mind and insert thoughts of you never leaving me, but it's clear to me that the "yes, no, maybe" factor has created a home in your heart. I wish I could blow up the memories of bullshit that you went through before me to give me an easier race, but instead, you choose to control my pace and keep the memory of being hurt by nonsense on a shelf to remind yourself that you're not worthy to be loved. I wish you could see what I see. I wish you could feel the way I feel when I look into your eyes, but my words are covered with second-guessing, and my actions are taken as friendly gestures. So, I come to grasp that you're ready for love, but in reality, you feel that you can't love; well, let me show you. Let me create a feeling to remove those negative incentives off the shelf and replace them with the glow that people see in you every day. As you sleep on my worth, I have no choice but to remove myself and replace me with the what-ifs or memories that you'll hold on to so you can search for a duplicate feeling. As easy as you may think it is, it is as difficult as forcing yourself to love me like you know you should; it's hard to do. So be clear on what you want from me, because loyalty comes with a price, and your actions have yet to be paid for. I'm expensive, so living in the moment is never good enough for perfection. So let's be nonfiction about how you feel, and let's not have my flaws put your feelings on hold, because you have flaws too. So as my walls tend to build an infrastructure around my heart and hire my soul as the architect to design a divine line between space and time, the blinders on your eyes are removed by your mistake for walking away from greatness.

# XXX

Let me open your legs like a porno mag. Get your
insides wet like the Nile River. Let me please you, not
tease you like I missed you. I've been away for some
weeks; you've been away for some months. So, when
we see each other, let's fuck like it's our first time.
Being with you blows my mind; so when I see you, let
me eat you. My stick feels so good while I'm stroking
you. Pull your hair so you can arch your back for me.
Making love will last for some hours, but after that's
done, I'll make you scream so you can call me daddy.
Choke you, spank you, let your waterfall cum down until
you can't take no more, and even then, I'll keep going
because in a few seconds, you'll be begging for more.

# THE FIXER

I'll take your woman away from you before you can blink and tell her you love her. Just call me "the Doctor," fixing broken pieces of hearts, sending black roses to women who are no good. Like thieves in the night, they take your pride and your purpose for prospering by courts on a child who you thought for certain you pulled out on. Giving medicine to women who crave for the prescription to be loved, not lied to, just to get in their pants. But the meds that I provide are to help ease their minds so they can find reasons to trust again, 'cause they been fucked over so many times, they don't even know if it's a lie or the truth; well, let me help you with that. Take a seat, and let me undress your mind. Take your dreams to another level so that when you look in the mirror, the reflection you'll see is me loving you. Denying those who only want the attention not to put in the work of loving me.

I'm a mystery, so it's clear to me why my ocean is filled with beautiful mermaids waiting for the bait to touch the surface. Giving certain women a sense of purpose to get a chance to be with a woman who'll boost their confidence and create an outlet that only one of them will keep.

# ADDICTED

Hi, my name is Real Thoughts ... And I'm addicted

to your mind. Your thoughts dressed as secrets

that I would love to undress and fuck.

Moments go unnoticed as you sleep, and I count the hairs

on your upper right eyebrow. I'm addicted to your fears

that capture the safety net of my bed of security.

So, the serenity of my outburst of my lust for your thoughts of

me, wondering what it is that you think of when you're deep in

thought—I hope it's me, naked enough so my soul is shown.

Giving you comfort to undress your soul, showing all your

imperfections, so that your heart receives my blanket of flaws

sewn with the needle and thread of redos 'cause no one is

perfect, but our minds put together can be perfection. I'm

addicted to how your mouth curves up before you speak. I wish

I could have a projection screen at my leisure every time you

come across my mind just to see your thoughts of the day.

I'm hungry for your internal opinion. What is the thought
that gets you in the mood? To think, where do you wanna
be in the next five years, why is your heart battered and
bruised, and why do you choose not to look me in the eye?
Who hurt you?
Let me take an ax and chop down every bit of
hurt that your memories tend to keep and create
dreams fallen into reality to fill the void.
I'm an addict of your past, present, and future thoughts,
so be my therapist and provide me with medicine
within your mind, not between your legs, because
between the sheets is where our souls unfold and our
inner obsessions are revealed into beautiful bliss.
Not only am I addicted to your mind, but I'm addicted to you.

# MY DAYDREAMS

I'm dreaming of an ocean full of mermaids

that I can barely touch.

My sense of taste is acquired; some may believe that

I may be square to bear their true desires, so they

draw back to what their taste buds are used to.

Others tend to linger to get what they feel they desire because of

past sharks that pretended to be lions. Well, I'm a rare breed,

Mixing in well with the others who try to fit in, but I

stay clear from the box that everyone gravitates to.

It's impossible for me to be duplicated. Some may call me

irrational, but I would rather be rational to the fact that it

takes a lot to get to know me. So, think what you want, and

see what your eyes intend for you to see. Instead, I seek

peace in every being I encounter. That's why positivity is

the energy and vibe that matches well with my cologne.

Imperfection is perfect to me. Maybe that's why your girl

is trying to creep. She wanna lie in my sheets while I give

her knowledge; crazy thing is she's a good thinker.

For twenty-four hours, she wanna change

her studies to lickilogy, but what the fuck

does that have to do with my mental?

Her zodiac sign doesn't match well with mine, so this situation

is crucial, but my critical thinking has got her head gone. Don't

know if she wanna stay or if she wanna leave, so I choose for

her and show her the door 'cause she's not willing to help me

cleanse my pain from the walls nor my depression from under

my bed. She just wanna lie in my sheets of passion, stripping

my sexual appetite for her own pleasures and not her desires.

# RELATIONSHIPS AND FAIRY TALES

I love you; that is the best way to describe how much

you mean to me. Every second I'm looking into your

eyes, my dreams become reality, full of the thought

of loving you. You're beautiful, not just how God

carved your outer features but on the inside.

He made sure that silver and gold were

a part of your heart and soul.

So in this cold world, I look for you to bring the sunshine

into my life, seeking for your touch within the darkness

of my nights. Keep your kisses tucked tight underneath

my pillow so when my head lies to rest, my mind can only

think of you. Some may call my hopes and dreams of real

love a fairy tale 'cause I'm single, hoping for my queen of

hearts to come and share my world and throne with me.

I'm so tired of wishy-washy women who don't know the

difference between real love and real tattoos. Looks are

only short term if you only look above the surface.

Real love is disguised in and around things we might not want to understand or believe. So, keep relationships away from me 'cause my fairy tale will become reality once my queen's conversation turns into needing instead of wanting. Wanting a relationship is not the same as needing a fairy tale. Relationships want you to do things you don't understand; fairy tales make you want to learn how to love and how to grow with someone who wants a fairy tale just as much as you need one.

# MONEY CAN'T BUY HAPPINESS

I know I don't have the cash to shower you with gifts that
you deserve, but I have the ability to do so. So, don't walk
away from perfection in the making; my struggle is my
hustle that keeps me humble. Silver spoons are for the weak
to believe everything that they have is theirs forever, but
forever is not in a day, so stay with me while I make my
own silver spoons and feed your mind off a golden plate.
My thoughts of you are occurring with ways
to spoil you, and not just material-wise; bills
and the ease of everything will be okay.
Friends are the beginning, but best friends and
marriage are what I'm trying to get to with you.
I don't have much now, but in due time, a listening ear plus
back rubs that soothe your body at night. I'm a human
who requires your attention, but if I'm not the flame

that catches your fire nor the beat that makes your heart skip, I'll be at peace with us just as friends and look out into the window from my window seat and dream of the day that you were supposed to take my last name.

# BONNIE AND CLYDE

Oblivious to the fact that we shouldn't have crossed lines to

become more than friends, but I wanted a Bonnie. Ready

to ride, pick up shell casings blown from my AK-47.

(Those are thoughts of being in power.) Putting money on the

jail phone 'cause the brick wall was trying to get the best of me.

Reaching for air on top of clouds. Searching for

freedom for three and a half months.

I think if she had the proper transportation back then, she

would have tried to break me out; instead, she paid for the

lawyer. How clutch was that? Kept money in my pocket

when lint was trying to make a home in the creases.

(Even though you didn't have enough for two, you made

sure I had more to spend.) Bonnie and Clyde is what

she said she wanted to be; so, I gave her just that. A

guarantee of pure loyalty. Reasons to love and not regret

her parents' disappointments. Which led to disapprovals

as soon as the ring came into play. So, as we unloaded

the thoughts and memories on the table, cleaning the

barrels and secret passageways of our closets of truth,

Knowing the fact that my loyalty was questionable

at the door due to prior attempts at her heart,

I was careless, also carefree of love. Didn't really want it

'cause it was never felt until my grandfather, who was my

father too (but you were there when I laid him to rest). It

was before that when I vowed to never hurt her, but the

only thing to prove was my loyalty through my actions.

Amazing how distrust was there but she remained by my side,

Being blindsided of her infidelity through smooth-talking

niggas paying based on conversation. The finesse was real,

taking trees and dead presidents and putting them in my

hands, making sure my path didn't cross with her street shit.

Guess that's the playa way to go. So,

what I wanted was a Bonnie.

A quiet beauty, but deadly if you looked into her eyes,

trapped and intertwined in her spell. I guess I was the only

one who had the power to see past the dangerous beauty;

realizing she was looking for Clyde, I gave her just that.

A hopeless romantic kinda Clyde was I, but roses and cute

suggestions only persuaded her attention for a moment.

Being frustrated at the fact she was never happy. Taking cold

shoulders, nonsexual nights to only give me the motivation

to have thoughts of a challenge. I enjoyed them, fighting

for something that I wanted, and I knew I could have it

just through the way she fed my ego. Only to be driven by

wild car chases of "Why can't you see I'm doing this for

the both of us?" Only to come to the focus that she was

preparing me to learn to love for myself, with myself.

She said I was fat; I got a gym membership. Started

paying attention to what went in my body, hoping that

she would take this journey with me, but only to fall

for scenes after she finished with scripts. (That's weed,

cigarettes, and oh, if her bitches didn't come through.)

Funny how two people can be in the same book

but on separate pages, different paragraphs, and

different sentences and remain as one.

Doubling back on the years that we had been in this war of

love. Feeling drained, strained, and all fucked up, taking

cover. Watching what moves I took to keep a smile on her

face. Faced with the hourglass damn near gone only to

come to face the reality that our four and a half years of love

were always based on six and a half years of pure loyalty.

# BLOOD AND WATER

Hope this poem doesn't piss any of my day ones off (that's family, friends, and foes included). Growing up for me was never peaches and cream. My grandfather always told me to chase after my dreams, and though my grandmother and aunt laughed at the original images of me dressed in army fatigues, it was three friends who told me I could do it. They introduced me to people who treated me like I was fam and taught me to use an outlet that I already had, more than an army of men could ever have. So, growing up for me was always searching for my purpose in life. Praying to God to give me a sign 'cause my search for a mother's love was always replaced with an aunt's love created to be a mother's love.

I'm lost pulling back to the streets 'cause home ain't home no more; even my big cousins lie to me, saying, "I got your back," but it all came back to three friends giving me shelter when a warrant was served.

I thank God for the King's mother because she
could've turned her back and denied me refuge, but
instead, she believed in the light she saw in me.
Treated me like I was her own.
So what's blood to water, and what's water to blood?
Both drip, but you need them both to survive. I guess
real love was tested when I got arrested; got one
visit from the two who laughed at my dreams.
Phoned home to my uncle, who drew up contracts of false
hope from first cousins, just to think, *Imma make bail.*
It was only with Grandmother's prayers, God's hand,
and the day my grandfather walked through the gates
of heaven that I was free to grieve. Guess some people
couldn't see outside the box but still have belief that I'll
be great. Still extending my hand to my mother, who was
always Momma to me. Trying to paint a perfect picture of
a perfect daughter in front of a church full of people.
Exceeding my ability in school just so I could have a mother
instead of a friend, but I guess the lifestyle that I choose—
to lie down with women—altered her judgment, or could
it have been the church folks' whispers of judgment?
I guess the treatment of arguments like strangers
needed to be in place to show I was still her child.

So, what's blood to water, and what's water to blood? Both

drip, but you need both to survive. Back in high school,

I was known all over as "That's my nigga!" My circle was

still small, even had two male best friends who hated

each other. Taught one how to get women and dress like

a man instead of a boy. I guess the distance between

us built a bush of fire filled with neglect, 'cause when I

needed him, I had to excuse his back for being present.

So, my day-one nigga was always disappearing and shit.

The death of his moms kept him lost for a while. He never

asked for friendly gestures, only actions of being real. It

wasn't till we got older that he realized that I was always

there. Had two female besties 'cause that's all I needed.

Knew one since the sixth grade, but my sixth

sense didn't work when she crossed me.

Thought my loyalty of being there in her time of need secured

a safety net of the knives she had for her other friends; I

guess she was just waiting for the opportunity to show.

Now as adults, we've slowed down; I'm glad now

we are able to get back to being true friends.

The other shares the lifestyle with me; I still

wonder why I was the last to know.

My wonder should have been when she would use my

name in vain to make a homie think I really needed her.

31

My energy to cheer for greatness for friends ended when I

couldn't get the same energy back behind closed doors.

Sad that our friendship never ended but just was left unsaid.

So, what's blood to water, and what's water to blood?

They both drip, but you need them both to survive.

# THE FALL

Embrace me with your thoughts of me never leaving
you. Comfort my soul with the essence of your presence.
Secure me with your way of uplifting me into falling
in love with you. I'm amused by your spirit.
So, let me create a silhouette of fantasies
that are made to turn into reality.
Write goals together, building a world nonbelievers are
searching for. Let us catch stars and make a potion to
be forever young. It's no secret that I'm falling for you,
but it is the love for you that will not let me fall.
Instead, I'll pour concrete into the cracks of your
heart, lick every inch of the bruises that hurt deep
within your soul, and with my tears, I'll wash the
memories away that made you shut down.
There's no secret that I'm falling for you and your love
for me will not let me fall. I'm careless at times, so my
line of work could sometimes be my work of art.

Isn't that what love is for? To work together; to build together? With just one touching the surface, it takes two to make one whole. So, I'll patiently wait for your heart to connect with mine, like Bluetooth. We may not sometimes see eye to eye, but if we continue to come closer, the connection will be priceless. So, don't leave me speechless, don't leave me broken without notice, because I'm scared too.

I'm falling for you, but it's the fall that I'm afraid of if you miss the catch. So forgive me if I show what love has made for me: a bed filled with possibilities of *could be*. Don't leave me wondering if the world that we started could be strong enough to hold down all the sacrifices that were made to keep us strong. Leave second thoughts and negative implements at the door of passion.

I'm falling for you, but my love that I have for you won't let me fall, so do us both a favor and let your love catch me instead of letting your mind make me fall.

# ONCE UPON A TIME

You're so beautiful; butterflies envy you. The
sun doesn't shine until you smile.
So, to me, you're perfect, and I know it's hard to believe, but
in my world, you share my throne with me. My heart is yours
for the taking because my eyes won't let you out of my sight.
Your lips feel so right when they're against mine.
I feel like a kid in a candy store the way
you give me what I desire.
Pleasure is the key that opens the door to our happily-
ever-after. Growing old together doesn't seem boring
to us because as long as we're together, it feels like
the very first time we laid eyes on each other.

# THE ONE

Staring at the clock, wishing my eyes would be laid on you.

Dealing with thoughts of not being able to feel your touch

kills me inside, but just in the nick of time, you appear

in my dreams, and from that point, I'm finally free.

You take care of my heart as if it were your own,

and for that, my soul will never be cold.

I miss you, baby, and the universe knows it; that's

why our minds are intertwined together.

So when the thought of me saying, "I love you,"

leaves me, I know in my heart that you'll hear it.

It breaks my heart because you can't see it.

Only at a moment's notice, we'll be back together

real soon, and my actions will show, instead of

words, to let you know I appreciate you.

# AGGRESSIVE POSITION

Your smile is remarkable with God's light that shines out when
your cheeks rise and your eyes close as you show your pretty
teeth as I make the laughter come out your mouth; that's my job.
Creating thoughts to make sure that you know your worth. Not
that I'm saying that you don't know, but what you think you're
worth, I believe that it's ten times more valuable than that.
I don't deserve you, and I'm not comfortable, so let
me do everything in my power to show you that I'm
worth your time. That's my job. My sexual orientation
has nothing to do with how I put my queen first.
I must be a triple threat to come correct 'cause my love is
passionate to intensify your everyday life. Small things mean
big things, so while a man tries to intensify your physical
state, I'll intensify you mentally, spiritually, and emotionally.
The physical side is just a bonus. I would love to enhance
inner thoughts because subconsciously you're already mine.
My only problem is I must wait till you catch up.

37

# ARGUMENTS AND SEX

I love to fight with you; it's the sexiest thing on earth. Now, this
may seem weird, but an argument with you makes me crave
for makeup sex 'cause I know that shit is going to be bomb.
No joke, I wanna choke you; push you into a wall while you
get in my face while we're looking intensely at each other.
I wanna kiss you passionately and tell you I hear
you. Pick you up, take your mind, throw it on the
floor, undress your anger, and please your ego.
Lick my apologies into your inner thigh,
whisper, "I'm sorry," in your ear.
I just wanna disagree for a minute. Take the time to get
to know new buttons just as well as old buttons.
Sex won't always work, but let me listen to your frustrations
and take them in. Spread your frown into a smile to

create a balance of understanding between me and you

'cause what frustrates you might just frustrate me too.

I love our arguments. They help me learn to love you more;

besides, what's something great without a struggle?

# IN DUE TIME

Red roses pull off the stem as the weather begins to break,

but seasons are months, and perfect memories turn into

years; it feels like the summertime when I look into your eyes,

and conversations fascinate me as long as we converse.

It feels like a lifetime, separating dislikes and

likes; talking boss shit got me feeling like you

could be the shit that I'm searching for.

Too early to tell, but I'm at the gate of my fate holding

the key to my heart, doubting if I'm actually making the

right decision, because a lot of potential gems are in my

back pocket. But your vibe matches mine so well.

I understand that you're scared—hell, I'm scared too—

but I'm willing to open up to the possibility that this

situation can really be life changing for good.

Now, I know my words might be a little slurred when I'm around

you, but I'm perfectly blind when you're near me, meaning only

you and I see clear; others may see black and white to me.

Your vibe makes my eyes concentrate on your glow.

Although we are not on the low, I want you to myself. Call

me selfish, but in due time, my forever will be you.

I'm nervous 'cause butterflies seem to always

find me when I hear your voice.

In due time, my hands in yours with *I dos* on our

tongues and our hearts will be forever.

# EMOTIONAL ROLLER COASTER

My grandmother on my father's side passed away a year
or two ago. I'm confused because I don't know how to feel
when I knew little of her, but she knew a lot about me. Never
said she was curious about where I was. Maybe she did.
Recently my father passed away without
giving the little girl in me answers.
I pray that God gets the answers that I have
been trying to grasp from both parties.
Lost one of my jobs to an almost-stable job; stress seems to
get the best of me as I pray every day that my girl doesn't
walk out on me or, better yet, kiss and sneak behind
my back because I can't help her pay rent. She saw the
glowup in me; I hope she stays around for my blowup.
Just found my purpose in life, and all along, it was a pen
and a piece of paper. Self-worth—respect for a favorable
opinion of myself. Hope my girl understands that.

Never had a mother's love, just a mother's friendship,

so what I'm searching for is for someone to love

me through it all. Got a phobia of people getting

close to me because my heart gets attached.

They duck off into their own light, so my

pathways have always been dark.

So I keep a flashlight of faith on standby to

see my next step; maybe that's why I can't see

clearly who truly is there for me or not.

I'm self-made, but the MAN won't let be great with a nine-

to-five. Day to day, I feel trapped in my own nightmare.

Searching for the right answers to turn a dollar into a million.

Life is chess, so why does everybody know

how to play checkers instead?

Guess that's the easy way out. The

microwaveable way to succeed.

I'm creeping around corporate America to sneak a

way in. I guess the realness of my life will open a side

door. Fighting wars because battles are a small part

of war, but to be a part of a culture that touches souls

and hearts of real reality—now that's golden.

Appreciating every day I get to wake up on the side of

my girl instead of in a nine-by-five cell. Took a drug test

the other day. Hoping that I'll pass because I'm truly a

hippie at heart. Stepping into other people's shoes to get

through a paragraph that I tend to draft. Drawing graphs

for a clear view of what my generation is going through.

At least me. I hope someone can agree with me.

Didn't get the sense of my own value or worth till my

grandfather died. Hope he's smiling down, being proud

of my growth and my appetite to never give up.

I wish he was around to lift my head up for me when I drop it.

Now all I have is myself to do that.

So much pressure on a young twenty-six-year-old

who's cold on the outside but warm and broken on

the inside. They say I'm clingy, so I step back.

They say I'm distant, so I try to hide.

Guess I can't please everybody, squeezing into a box they

try to put me in. I'm uncomfortable; maybe that's why I'm

always breaking out. I just might be ahead of my time with

this poetry shit, 'cause most poets only gonna write about the

world tragedies and possibilities of fake love, not seeing and

feeling at the same time with your eyes through your heart.

The knowledge I have to offer is self-experienced.

I grew up around gangsters, so I became one. Everybody

has to have armor in this world, right? In my case,

my weapons have been words to pierce your mind

and your heart; I guess that's why I'm emotional.

# SEX WITH ME

I'm a Leo. So, my passion matches my sex drive.

If you stroke my ego well enough, I'll blow your mind.

I'm a mind freak, so our conversations have to have my

intellect amazed. I tend to spend most of my days searching,

trying to find someone who will keep my interest.

Sometimes I may slow down my words and my actions

as my eyes take the time to show and watch.

I got an anger problem. I fix it through writing

and fucking; so, sex with me is intense.

I'm consistent with finding a woman who can't tame this

cool-ass lioness. Conversations always fall off. I guess

I gotta carry convos like a ball hog on the court. I lose

focus on walking if I'm always thinking about a topic.

I'm fun size, so I like to climb tall trees. I'm underrated

in the bedroom till it's time for me to show and prove.

My stamina increases with your body movements. So, my

sex improves once moans make improvements in my ear.

My sex is a gift, so my body count is limited.

I'm not just a confident sex addict. I'm confident that

I am addicted to sex. My voice alone can make your

pussy cum before my tongue licks your inner thigh.

I come in clutch like a breath of fresh air. I can be your weekend

lover if you let me bend you over and make you call me daddy.

I'll make sure my application stays on file only if

you need me for a little while. Scratch my back

just like how your day was. Long and rough.

I'll make sure my strokes are felt deep within your ocean.

I ain't shady, but I got more than fifty ways, and they ain't

gray faded to black but bright colors. So, seduction alone

is the color fire, but me soothing your flame is my aim.

Visions of my stroke in the mirror are not a factor when your

eyes are rolling in the back of your head. I'm very smart,

so the knowledge that I provide eases a woman's mind.

Hope you don't go to work the next day; calling

off is on the agenda if need be. My sex requires

recovery days of warm milk and honey baths.

I'll leave you in daze. I talk shit, but I can back my shit

up. That's how you walk and talk at the same time.

Let me eat you from the back. Pussy is my favorite

food; so when I say, "I'm hungry," all I want is you

on the menu or on a counter, or a chair, maybe

even the floor. Might not reach the bed.

Let me set a reminder to remind your body that

it belongs to me. I wanna wake your pussy up by

reading a text saying, "Grand Rising Queen."

I enjoy pillow talk. Anything that I can

work on to please you better.

I'm trying to learn new tricks. I'm willing to

take the risk and make a movie with you.

I'm a freak, so sending me naked pictures and booty videos gets

you the five-star treatment to amazing treats and great sex.

I'm random and let you know what's on my mind ahead

of time by my movements. My hands you have to forgive

for pulling down your pants, shooting a text saying,

"Panties off," and looking at you like I wanna eat you.

My bite is just as smooth as a roar that

comes off the tip of my tongue.

So sex with me, bottom line, is always amazing.

Forget positions; I wanna position your mind to

the motion of you bending over, letting me hit it

from the back. Only if you have sex with me.

# TEMPTATION ISLAND

I've been on this island where the

women are beautiful naturally.

Truly my eyes have turned into tunnel vision, and my

eyelids have not blinked since they laid on you.

Expectations were low, but when I was with

you, my temptations were high.

I blow your mind with impure actions as conversations tend to

engage in touching with our hands. Feeling in paradise when

I'm embraced by your presence, being filled with the curse

of women on this island makes my imperfections unseen.

Clearly you enjoy my confidence.

Could it be the luck I have on this island is fifty-fifty? The half

that's good is probably you. Even your other half is bad luck

because of false hope. The key to your heart belongs to another.

It leaves me at the gate, pounding my soul on the bottom

of my shoes. I'm tucking the temptation I have for you

tightly under the palm of my hand. So I don't create a

plot to steal what I feel belongs to me. Being the other

woman is something that has had its perks, unquestionable

destinations. I do not have to answer when you call.

My house is not yours, nor my bed. No matter how many times

your beauty has touched my pillow, you are still not mine.

So the intentions of me coming home at a designated time

are thin. I have no rules, no boundaries, but you still tend

to knock on my door at times when clearly the person

who holds the key to your heart is always unavailable.

You show up with see-through lace of

sexual intentions of romance.

The look of sexual advances, damn, you so fine.

Trying to look past seduction through your bra.

I know it's wrong, but it feels so right, but I can't give in.

So, I offer change. A penny for your thoughts, a nickel for

a kiss, and a dime for your heart, but instead, I got your

ass in the air, connected to your moans calling for me.

My name sounds so good when it's after your moans.

If I could escape this island, my legs would stay stagnant

firmly in the sand 'cause I can't fight temptation.

# A TASTE OF AFFECTION

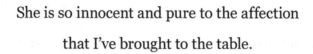

She is so innocent and pure to the affection

that I've brought to the table.

So, she hides her true feelings within, just as I begin

to unfold past attempts of loving genuinely.

Effortlessly I tend to push away something so pure as her.

Just got out of a relapse of getting my heart broken. Guess

I attract the foolery and not the purity that she brings.

As we began to acknowledge we are alike, as broken hearts

reflected off each other, we began to flirt within time. I began

to love her, and by the same token, she began to love me as we

both began to second-guess our friendship that got us here.

Knowing she'll take care of my heart that beats to keep the

little life I have for love alive, I still haven't sewn all the pieces

back together; I'm tarnished yet am still saying that I'm willing

to try something so sweet to me but brand new to her.

Saying, "I love you," was so right and easy, but saying, "I'm

in love with you," would be a risk 'cause my heart can't

deal with pain, especially if the pain is not worth feeling.
But for her, I'm willing to drill another hole in my soul to
take a chance that she just might be worth the pain.
Sometimes I wonder if I can take a slice of cake and eat
it too; by the way, she spoils me with her affection.
Can't even deny the attraction between us as we send
"I miss you" through text at the same time.
Comfort is what she is to me because I'm in a zone of just
loving her; as a friend, that is. In my past love life, I was
mistreated by accident. Letting past lovers get tripped up
by karma. Learning that I was a lesson toward subjects
that they couldn't pass due to shit that they were used to.
Wondering if love is really in my corner, instead of dragging
her into misunderstood confusion, I let her stay as my main ...
friend. The one I flirt with, spend time with, share secrets
with that I'm uncomfortable to say in front of strangers.
My boo that no one can replace. And as much as I would
love to taste her, I won't until she states otherwise.
So, I will sit on the phone with the love that I can't
call my own and wait for a taste of her affection.

# BLUNTS AND KISSES

I'm a hippie. So, let my peace be, that my lips gently roll this sativa into this raw cone. Letting the natural smoke hit your lungs naturally 'cause naturally, I fuck with you. No need to chop your trees 'cause I got plenty for the both of our planes to take flight.

All I want is blunts and kisses. Let's take time to slow time down with a bong of possibilities. I just want you next to me. Let the exotic smoke cuddle us into each other's arms. Lie on clouds with tunes of Jhene and Sade soothing our souls. Grinding keef, rolling it into a wood as I persuade that you should spend the night because honestly, I just want blunts and your kisses. Break the kush down and mix it with the indica 'cause I'm really feeling the vibe that we share when we're alone.

So, let's be bold and let the dark white smoke take us to cloud nine 'cause honestly, I just want blunts and your kisses.

# CAN'T LET GO

Yesterday, I called you, but I didn't get an answer.

Instead, I sat on the phone, listening to your voicemail just to

capture your voice, envisioning you saying my name. As I hung

up before it beeped, my nerves wouldn't allow me to call back, or

for that matter leave a message just to let you know I miss you.

I can't let go of you.

I can't let go.

Walking past the hourglass with the reflection

of your body's image behind me.

My love for you is genuine.

So how can we say goodbye to each other when

our hearts are considered to be one?

I can't let go.

Letting go for me is letting go of the tree that we

planted together, uprooting roots that we're unsure

will survive on their own. So I'll take the roots of

my soul and put them into the ocean of hope.

I'll send a search party for your heart 'cause

I can't let go.

# IF I WAS YOURS

Both hearts belong to others, but we both second-guess,

asking for our freedom. I belong to her, seeking her time

at the end of the day but only left with voicemails saying

her attendance will be late. Having leftovers of guilt.

I'm beginning to lose myself.

You belong to him. Never dealt with a woman before, but when

I opened the door for you and called you beautiful, the door

of curiosity was opened. You see, consistency is key with me.

The things he used to do he doesn't do anymore. Just goes

to show you he got comfortable when he knew he had you.

His appeal doesn't appease your eye anymore. His

actions in romance ended quickly. Your infatuation

with me has grown. If I were yours, your self-esteem

wouldn't need makeup for Snapchat filters.

My love is natural, so naturally, I see your beauty naturally.

I love what I see.

Your soul keeps me speechless, and your heart

is beginning to brighten up my destiny.

# JUST SAY YES

Can I kiss every intimate thought that

processes through your mind—

The thoughts that attract your body parts to take part in

action so I can give you satisfaction between your thighs?

I just want to taste your forbidden water as my

hands caress the rest of your body. My tricks are

exclusive, but my taste buds crave you … Shh …

Just say yes.

Say yes to the drip that leads a trail from the footsteps of my

tongue to where the tip is in touch with your walls of paradise.

Shit! You taste good.

I'd rather be in prison within a memory you unlock every

moment you think of me. I want you and every part of you.

I need permission to become the savage you fantasize about

So as to unleash your wild side to vibe with the lion within me.

Let my voice undress the best intellectual

thought your mind has to offer me.

Speechless is what I want the best part of your night

through the morning to be, so please just say yes.

# UNTOUCHABLE

As we connect with our eyes and our

hands are intertwined as one

And our dreams begin to end as reality

sets in, becoming our dream,

Untouchable is what we are.

Separating our wants and focused on our needs, helping

one another to grow is the game plan for eternity.

So we both take turns being our coach,

Sitting bench players out in the nosebleeds,

Keeping gossip, rumors, and jealous situations out of our

mental because our communication is one hundred.

So, what's mine is yours, and what's yours is mine.

Together, our love story never has to end.

With skin to skin being unbroken, when we

kiss, our intimacy is untouchable to outsiders

because our hands crave for only our touch.

Printed in the United States
By Bookmasters